A PROSE ANTHOLOGY
OF THE
SECOND WORLD WAR

Selected and edited by Robert Hull

Wayland

Prose Anthologies of War

A Prose Anthology of the First World War

A Prose Anthology of the Second World War

First published in 1992 by
Wayland (Publishers) Ltd
61 Western Road, Hove
East Sussex BN3 1JD

Editor: Cath Senker
Designer: David Armitage
Picture editor: Michael Cardona
Consultant: John Rowley, history advisory teacher at the South-west Divisional Professional
Centre, Southampton

British Cataloguing in Publication Data

A Prose Anthology of the Second World War. –
(Prose Anthologies of the World Wars series)
 I. Hull, Robert II. Series
 940.54

ISBN 0 7502 0453 2

Typeset by Dorchester Typesetting Group Ltd, Dorchester
Printed and bound by Butler and Tanner Ltd, Frome and London, England

Picture acknowledgements

Communist Party Library 13; Imperial War Museum 8, 9, 15, 17, 20, 22, 29, 33, 34, 35, 39, 42, 44,
45, 51, 53, 54, 55, 57; Mansell 7; Popperfoto 7, 32, 36, 37, 58; The Research House 30, 31, 38;
Topham *contents page*, 5, 12, 14, 16, 19, 23, 24, 26, 27, 43, 47, 49, 52; Wayland Picture Library 6,
18, 28.

Contents

Introduction

Sometimes, reading history, we learn about events without understanding what it was like for people living through them. The idea of this collection is to convey some of the individual experience that lies behind 'the facts'. Reading general history books is like seeing what happened from a long way off; you could compare it with looking down at the Earth from a satellite in orbit. This satellite view is one which we need, but if we want to know what the war was like for individuals, what really happened to people in history, we need to go down closer and to listen to their stories, and try to imagine our way into their lives.

Even when you think you know about some aspect of history, your knowledge can fade, or become vague. The stories and words of individuals refresh your awareness. When I read the letter which Dr A. received in 1933, removing him, because he was a Jew, from the panel of practising doctors – even though two of his sons had died fighting for Germany – I felt a small, valuable shock; 'Yes, that's what it must have been like.' I already knew about the treatment of the Jews, but I did not know about Dr A. Now he is a necessary part of my understanding.

It also increases our awareness to hear the voices of people who will shock us. Perhaps we have read about the 'concentration camps' and tried to imagine their unimaginable terrors. To read the horrific words of Heinrich Himmler, or any of those who created and ran the camps, helps us to understand something hardly understandable.

Because this book is made up of the words of individual people, it cannot tell the story of the war. Although it is history, it is not 'a history'. What we have tried to do is to include a wide range of experiences, and represent as many nationalities and roles as possible: Japanese soldier, American nurse, Polish schoolboy, German air force pilot, French pastor, British politician, and so on.

Even that short list suggests that it was a 'world' war, not a single war. It developed from two large wars that became tangled together, and which then produced several other wars as more countries joined in on one side or the other.

At first, the war in Europe was between Germany and just two other nations, Britain and France. Then it spread as Adolf Hitler invaded other countries, conquering large areas of Europe. The second war was that between Japan and China, and then other nations of the Pacific. Like Hitler's supporters, Japan's militaristic rulers thought their country was too small and crowded, and needed more room. The two large wars became one when the United States fleet in Pearl Harbor, on Hawaii, was attacked by Japan. The United States then declared war against Japan. In return, Japan's ally, Germany, declared war on the USA.

Thirty million people died in the Second World War. Most were civilians, and large numbers of those, Japanese and German and British, died in bombing raids aimed directly at them. More Japanese civilians died than members of the armed forces. Millions of Jews died, deliberately murdered, or slowly killed by starvation in the concentration camps and ghettos. One million Greeks, out of a population of eight million, died of hunger.

Sometimes we need to go back to experiences in the singular to make sense of these huge numbers. The war was the millions of dead, but it was also a few frightened Japanese villagers arguing about the length of spears needed to repel the coming Americans. It was some German students protesting about Hitler's crimes. It was a French pastor, under orders to gather Jews together ready for deportation, saying: 'We do not know what a Jew is. We know only men.'

THE NAZIS AND THE JEWS

Hitler and the Nazis believed that the Germans were a superior 'Aryan race'. Aryans were blond, blue-eyed and tall – although many Germans did not fit this description. According to this belief, the Aryan race was destined to rule the world by subduing all the other races. In Germany, this meant, among other things, eliminating the Jews.

Several years before the 1939–45 war began, Jews were being discriminated against in Germany – in other words, punished – for being Jews. One method was to prevent Jews from working at their usual occupations. This happened to Dr Hans A., two of whose sons had died in the 1914–18 war. In 1915 he had received this letter.

THURINGIAN Field Artillery Regt. No. . . . .
2nd Battery   In the Field, *16th June, 1915.*
To:
Staff Medical Officer Dr A.,
Infantry Regt. No. . . .
In the Field.
DEAR DR A.,

The battery regrets to have to inform you that your son, Volunteer N.C.O. Kurt A., died a hero's death for the Fatherland on the morning of June 13th. He fell defending the gun entrusted to his care. With you the battery mourns the death of this exemplary and courageous comrade. May God help you to bear this pain and give you comfort.

                                                     With deepest respect,

                                                     . . . .
                                                     Captain Commanding Battery [1]

This letter came for Dr A. in 1933.

Admission Committee for the
Medical District of . . .
Health Insurance.   *1st June, 1933.*
To:
Dr Hans A.
DEAR SIR,

I have to inform you that as a non-Aryan without the qualification of service at the front you have been removed from panel practice.

You are to refrain from all participation in panel practice. Your accounts will no longer be settled. Your attention is expressly drawn to the inevitable consequences of failure to adhere strictly to these instructions.

Heil Hitler!

. . . .
Chairman of Admission Committee.[2]

The war began in September 1939, after Germany invaded Poland. France, Holland, Belgium and Luxembourg were conquered the following May. In countries that were taken over by the Germans, Jews were – literally – labelled, by being forced to wear a yellow star. Marie-Christine Gouin was eight when the war began. She lived in Paris with her family. Her mother was Jewish, but not her father.

My mother was Jewish and had to wear a yellow star. My sister and I were classed as Aryans by the Germans so we didn't have to. Thank goodness my sister and I did not have to wear that yellow star. Our friends who did were horribly taunted. My mother like all Jews had to submit to humiliating restrictions which she bore with great dignity. Not only was she forbidden to leave Paris, she wasn't even allowed to go out after 8 o'clock at night. Despite all this my mother tried to make our lives as normal as possible. It was only after the war that I realized how much she must have suffered and how much her health had been harmed by all the stress she had endured.

Many of her friends and relations were sent to the concentration camps and she lived in dread of a knock at the door. But she had a friend in the police who would often warn her not to enter certain Metro stations on a particular day as the Germans planned to search them for Jews to send away.[3]

The Nazis forced Jews from all over Europe to go to concentration camps. But there were some protests from non-Jews. Pastor André Trocmé, who helped Jews in Le Chambon, southern France, described in his notes how he argued with the local Prefect against carrying out orders to deport them.

Prefect Bach replied, 'It is true that I have already received orders and that I shall put them into effect. Foreign Jews who live in the Haute-Loire are not your brothers. They do not belong to your church, nor to your country! Besides, it is not a question of deportation.'

Trocmé asked, 'What, then, is it a question of?'

'My information comes from the marshal himself. And the marshal does not lie! The Führer is an intelligent man. Just as the English have created a Zionist centre in Palestine, the Führer has ordered the regrouping of all European Jews in Poland. There they will have land and houses. They will lead a life that is suitable for them, and they will cease to corrupt the West. In a few days my people will come to examine the Jews living in Le Chambon.'

Trocmé replied, 'We do not know what a Jew is. We know only men.'[4]

Prefect *Head of the police force.*
Zionist centre in Palestine *Refers to the decision by Britain to permit a limited number of Jews to settle in Palestine.*

When the Nazis occupied Poland, the Jews in each town were rounded up and herded into one place. The Jews called these areas the ghettos. Gradually the ghetto population was reduced, as the Nazis sent the Jews to concentration camps. There they lived in squalor, with very little food. Ben Helfgott was a schoolboy in Piotrkow, Poland, when the war broke out. He was sent to Buchenwald camp.

They gave us stinking soup – it really smelt like sewage; and there was no salt; although we were very hungry, we simply couldn't eat this soup. But the prisoners who were already there got wind of this, and they came over to us. They were skeletons, teeming with lice – the very sub-humans the Germans maintained that we Jews were. And they fought each other for the soup. One of the cauldrons was overturned and they fell on the ground, licking the liquid from the dirty floor.

We were appalled at these people, but I tell you that within two days we were eating that soup with them, and the only thing we thought was how foolish we had been to let our first ration go.[5]

Alexander Donat, a Pole who survived the Warsaw ghetto and the concentration camps, and wrote a book about his experiences, recounted a moment of protest and support from a German civilian outside the camp.

One day while I was digging in the quarry alone, a German civilian walked by, stopped and stood about a hundred yards away from me. Suddenly, in the unnatural silence, he began to whistle the first bars of the *Internationale.* 'Arise ye prisoners of starvation, arise ye wretches of the earth . . .' So struck was I by this song of international solidarity in that pit of hatred that when he stopped, I whistled the second verse. When I stopped, he picked up the third verse, and so our whistled dialogue continued until the anthem was finished. On his way out, when he passed by me, he smiled and whispered, 'Keep your chin up. We're not all like them. We'll help you.' He said something else, but it was in Swabian dialect and I couldn't understand him. I never saw him again.[6]

Internationale *A revolutionary socialist hymn.*

Jews within the ghettos eventually resisted the Nazis, although it was a case of too little, too late. In April 1943, the Jewish Armed Resistance Organization, recently formed in the Warsaw ghetto, issued this appeal to the Polish people:

Poles, citizens, soldiers of Freedom! Through the din of German cannon, destroying the homes of our mothers, wives and children; through the noise of their machine-guns, seized by us in the fight against the cowardly German police and SS men; through the smoke of the Ghetto, that was set on fire, and the blood of its mercilessly killed defenders, we, the slaves of the Ghetto, convey heartfelt greetings to you.

We are well aware that you have been witnessing breathlessly, with broken hearts, with tears of compassion, with horror and enthusiasm, the war that we have been waging against every brutal occupant these past few days.

Every doorstep in the Ghetto has become a stronghold and shall remain a fortress until the end! All of us will probably perish in the fight, but we shall never surrender! We, as well as you, are burning with the desire to punish the enemy for all his crimes, with a desire for vengeance. It is a fight for our freedom, as well as yours; for our human dignity and national honour, as well as yours! We shall avenge the gory deeds of Oswiecim, Treblinka, Belzec and Majdanek!

Long live the fraternity of blood and weapons in a fighting Poland!
Long live freedom!
Death to the hangman and the killer!
We must continue our mutual struggle against the occupant until the very end![7]

Many Germans were appalled at the evil they saw. In 1942 a group of Munich students wrote a fierce pamphlet of protest. They were all executed.

Why does the German people show such apathy towards all these frightful and inhuman crimes? Hardly anyone seems to trouble about them. They are accepted as facts and put aside, and the German people falls again into its dull obtuse sleep, giving these Fascist criminals the courage and the opportunity to continue their havoc – and they take it. Can this be a sign that the Germans have been blunted in their deepest human feelings, that no chord in them vibrates when they hear of such deeds, that they have sunk into a deadly sleep from which there can never, never, be an awakening? It seems so, and it certainly will be so unless the Germans awake at last from their stupor, unless they seize every opportunity to protest against this criminal gang, unless they suffer with the hundreds of thousands of victims.[8]

The governments of European countries which had not been invaded by Hitler did little to support the Jews in Nazi-occupied areas. In Luxembourg, 2,000 Jews had been told by the Nazis to leave. Luxembourg asked whether Britain could accept them, or send them elsewhere in the British Empire, such as Tanganyika in Africa.

I am afraid there is next to nothing we can do. They are covered by the Home Office prejudice . . . against people from enemy-occupied territory: and in any case we simply cannot have any more people let into the United Kingdom on merely humanitarian grounds . . . Furthermore these particular refugees, pitiable as is their plight, are hardly war-refugees in the sense that they are in danger because they have fought against the Germans, but simply racial refugees.

T R Latham, minute of meeting at the British Foreign Office, 16 December 1940.[9]

The Nazis did not just impose a regime of cruelty on Jews. Conquered civilian populations were also dealt with brutally, as cold-blooded Nazi communications demonstrated. Heinrich Himmler, chief of the SS, made his views clear.

What happens to a Russian, or to a Czech, does not interest me in the slightest. What the nations can offer in the way of good blood of our type we will take, if necessary by kidnapping their children and raising them here with us. Whether nations live in prosperity or starve to death interests me only in so far as we need them as slaves for our *Kultur*: otherwise, it is of no interest to me. Whether ten thousand Russian females fall down from exhaustion while digging an anti-tank ditch interests me only in so far as the anti-tank ditch for Germany is finished.

Himmler, October 1943.[10]

FIGHTING IN WESTERN EUROPE

In May 1940 the German armies invaded Holland, Belgium and Luxembourg. The British, French and Belgian armies retreated to the area around Dunkirk, on the French coast. A thousand ships, mainly small ones, brought back about 300,000 troops to England. Field Marshal von Runstedt, the German Commander-in-Chief, gave his view of Dunkirk.

To me Dunkirk was one of the great turning-points of the war. If I had had my way the English would not have got off so lightly at Dunkirk. But my hands were tied by direct orders from Hitler himself. While the English were clambering into the ships off the beaches, I was kept uselessly outside the port unable to move. I recommended to the Supreme Command that my five Panzer divisions be immediately sent into the town and thereby completely destroy the retreating English. But I received definite orders from the Führer that under no circumstances was I to attack, and I was expressly forbidden to send any of my troops closer than ten kilometres from Dunkirk. The only weapons I was permitted to use against the English were my medium guns. At this distance I sat outside the town, watching the English escape, while my tanks and infantry were prohibited from moving.[11]

Panzer *Fast, mechanized armoured tanks.*

Pascal Jardin recalls in his book how, as a young boy, he heard news of the defeat of France in June 1940.

16th June. A gloomy lunchtime. In the dining-room of the over-full hotel, extreme tension prevailed. At three o'clock the loudspeaker of the radio announced that Marshal Pétain was going to make a solemn appeal. Everyone stood up: 'Men and women of France, from today I shall take over the leadership of the French government . . .' As he spoke, faces froze . . . 'Last night I approached our adversary to ask, as between soldiers, whether he was prepared to join with us, after the battle and in all honour, in bringing an end to hostilities . . .' And then many people started crying, standing there crowded together in that seaside hotel dining-room. A very old gentleman who had been unable to get to his feet crumpled up and hid his face in his hands. My father was white as a sheet. I asked him what had happened. He answered softly:

'We have lost the war.' [12]

From 1940 to 1944, the Germans ruled France. It was not until June 1944 that Allied soldiers returned, to invade northern France. Guy Remington, an American paratrooper, described jumping into the Normandy night.

The green light flashed on at seven minutes past midnight. The jump master shouted, 'Go!' I was the second man out. The black Normandy pastures tilted and turned far beneath me. The first German flare came arching up, and instantly machine-guns and forty-millimetre guns began firing from the corners of the fields, striping the night with yellow, green, blue, and red tracers. I pitched down through a wild Fourth of July. Fire licked through the sky and blazed around the transports heaving high overhead. I saw some of them go plunging down in flames. One of them came down with a trooper, whose parachute had become caught on the tailpiece, streaming out behind. I heard a loud gush of air: a man went hurtling past, only a few yards away, his parachute collapsed and burning. Other parachutes, with men whose legs had been shot off slumped in the harness, floated gently toward the earth.

I was caught in a machine-gun cross fire as I approached the ground. It seemed impossible that they could miss me. One of the guns, hidden in a building, was firing at my parachute, which was already badly torn; the other aimed at my body. I reached up, caught the left risers of my parachute, and pulled on them. I went into a fast slip, but the tracers followed me down. I held the slip until I was about twenty-five feet from the ground and then let go the risers. I landed up against a hedge in a little garden at the rear of a German barracks.

There were four tracer holes through one of my pants' legs, two through the other, and another bullet had ripped off both my breast pockets, but I hadn't a scratch.

I fought behind the German lines for eight days before I was relieved by our seaborne troops.[13]

Fourth of July *On 4 July Americans celebrate the anniversary of independence with firework displays.*

In August 1944, after two months of fierce fighting, the Nazi forces pulled back. A British soldier, R M Wingfield, saw some German soldiers who had surrendered.

They came on, shambling in dusty files. Every few yards there was a single British infantryman. Even that guard was unnecessary. The shuffling wrecks just followed the Bren carrier in the lead. They were past caring. The figures were bowed with fatigue, although they had nothing to carry but their ragged uniforms and their weary, hopeless, battle-drugged bodies.[14]

British and US troops had invaded Sicily in July 1943. Walter Bernstein describes how he and other American soldiers captured the village of Ficarra. There were many Americans whose families had come from Italy; Caruso was one of them.

The road curved again and the houses thinned out still further. As we came around this curve, we saw two civilians running from a house that stood off by itself. They disappeared before we could do anything. We all stopped and looked at the closed door of the house. The house was a two-storey affair, with a large wooden door and no windows. Riley dropped to one knee, aiming his rifle at the door. Sheehan aimed his tommy gun. No one talked. I moved quietly up to the door and stood at one side of it, with my back against the house. Taylor moved over to take my place and covered the door. As soon as all the men were in position, I reached over and slowly tried the knob. The door was locked. I pressed against it very slowly, but it wouldn't give. I looked back at Riley, who nodded, and then I banged the door very hard with my gun. Almost immediately a woman began to cry inside. I banged again and she cried louder, and then she began to yell and shriek. I couldn't understand a word she said. She was yelling at the top of her lungs and all I could tell was that she was speaking Italian. *'Tedeschi?'* I asked, giving the Italian word for the Germans.

'No,' the woman screamed. *'No! No!'*

I looked over at Riley and he shrugged. He stood up and called for Caruso, who came running up. He motioned Caruso to the house and Caruso came over and stood at the other side of the door. The woman was still screaming and Caruso had to shout to make himself heard. Finally he yelled something in Italian that sounded very fierce and the woman shut up. For a moment there was no sound. Then the knob turned and the door slowly opened. A thin, middle-aged woman with stringy black hair stuck her head out. She looked first at me, then at Caruso. *'Americano?'* she asked. We nodded and Caruso said something in Italian. The woman looked at us again and then at the other soldiers in the street. She began to cry. She held her hands to her face and cried, and then she went over to Caruso and threw her arms around him and kissed him on both cheeks.[15]

REFUGEES AND 'ALIENS'

At the start of the war, about 10,000 Jewish children in Europe had been sent away by their parents to other countries, including Britain. German adults living in Britain were brought along to help the young refugees through customs. Norbert Wollheim realized that one of them was over the age limit of eighteen.

He had just been released from Dachau and his head was shaven. I asked him when he was born and sure enough he was over eighteen. He looked it; he was tall and broad. There was no way he could have been much younger. But I told him that whatever happened he had to say that he was born in 1924, three years on from his real birthday. At Harwich the immigration officer called me over. The boy was standing there, shaking. 'Ask him how old he is', said the immigration officer. The boy was word perfect. 'He says he was born in 1924', I translated. The officer looked at me, he looked at the boy. There was a long silence. Then he said to me, 'If there is an error, do you take responsibility?' Of course, I agreed. We were in.[16]

Dachau One of the concentration camps in Germany.

A great number of European Jewish children stayed in England for the rest of their lives. Many things were difficult at the beginning, including the new language. One young boy, now called Leslie Brent, described their new lives on the radio, in his new language.

A bell rings at eight o'clock and we have to get up. Some boys get up earlier to make a run to the sea which is near the camp. At 8.30 we have a good English breakfast, which we enjoy. First we did not eat porridge but now we like it. When we finish the breakfast we get the letters or cards from our parents, and then we are all very happy. After that we clear and tidy our rooms, then we have two hours lessons in English. When the lessons are over we take our lunch and then we can make what we like. After tea we can go to the sea, which is wonderful, or we play English games of football. In the evening we learn a lot of English songs till we go to bed. I sleep with two other boys in a nice little house. Now it is very cold and we cannot stay in our house. We like to sit around the stove in a very large hall, and we read or write to our parents. The people are very kind to us. A gentleman invited me to go with him in a car; then we drove to his house and there we had tea. Oh, it was very nice. Sometimes we go to a picture house in Dovercourt. We have seen the good film *Snow White and the Seven Dwarfs*. We were all delighted. Now I will go to school, then I can speak English good and then I would like to become a cook. We are all very happy to be in England.[17]

There were many Germans living in Britain at the start of the war. Amongst them, some politicians thought, there was a hidden 'Fifth Column Menace', a spy network. Sir Nevill Bland, the British Ambassador who had returned from Holland, believed this.

Every German or Austrian servant, however superficially charming and devoted, is a real and grave menace, and we cannot conclude from the experiences of the last war that 'the enemy in our midst' is no more dangerous than it was then. I have not the least doubt that when the signal is given, as it will scarcely fail to be when Hitler so decides, there will be satellites of the monster *all over the country* who will at once embark on widespread sabotage and attacks on civilians and the military indiscriminately. We cannot afford to take this risk. *All* Germans and Austrians, at least, ought to be interned at once.[18]

By summer 1940, the British Prime Minister, Winston Churchill, was in favour of deporting 'aliens'.

Has anything been done about shipping 20,000 internees to Newfoundland or St Helena? Is this one of the matters that the Lord President has in hand? If so, would you please ask him about it. I should like to get them on the high seas as soon as possible, but I suppose considerable arrangements have to be made at the other end. Is it all going forward?

Memorandum to Cabinet Secretary, 3 June 1940 [19]

Newfoundland A province in Canada; **St Helena** *An island in the Atlantic Ocean.*

Canada and Australia each volunteered to take several thousands of refugees. Soon the *Duchess of York* sailed for Canada and the *Arandora Star* for Australia. On 2 July 1940 the *Arandora Star* was torpedoed, and hundreds died when it sank. Alfred Cooper, a refugee himself, was on the *Arandora Star* and then the *Dunera*, which sailed for Australia on 10 July.

They didn't tell me that I was going to Australia, they just put me on the boat in Liverpool and off we went. We had trouble on the *Dunera*

. . . the guards used to urinate in the porridge; we all had dysentery. I think five people died. It was so crowded that some people used to sleep in hammocks and some on the mess tables. There were no proper toilets on the ship – there was one long board with different holes and water flushed all the time and of course that made the dysentery worse . . .

We were kept down below all the time but once a day they used to take us for a walk. We were behind barbed wire . . . I saw Table Mountain at Cape Town – everyone was allowed a minute at the port-hole. We were not allowed off the boat until Australia.

The man in charge of the men who guarded us was Captain O'Neill. He had the VC from the First World War. He used to rob the rich Jews. I saw him do it myself. When I first got on the boat the first thing I saw was a lot of suitcases opened. They used to beat us and tell us to hurry up and they would rip open the suitcases with their bayonets. Everybody made a claim when they got off the boat. My brother made a claim and the War Office repaid him for everything he had lost.

The *Dunera* was very bad. There were suicides. One of them walked in front of me and just jumped overboard. And one person got killed in a fight over a hammock.[20]

VC Victoria Cross, a medal for great bravery in war.

BOMBING THE CITIES

In 1940 Hitler wanted to invade Britain. In preparation, he planned to bomb factories, air force and military installations, and if necessary, British civilians. The massed planes of the *Luftwaffe* bombed London continuously through the autumn and winter of 1940.

Dorothy Barton worked as a typist in the day, and as a fire-watcher at night. During one air raid, her own house was hit.

As I turned towards our house a few yards away I heard Dad talking to someone I couldn't see, then I pushed open our front door and went inside. I'd hardly got into the passage when there was a tremendous explosion and our house rocked sideways, while windows, ceiling and doors flew about. I managed to throw myself into the living room, where I was dragged under the table by my mother, who was sheltering there with the younger children.

A few minutes later there was another explosion and the house rocked the other way, accompanied by the crash of still more falling debris, both inside and out. Soon afterwards Dad ran in, grabbed the cloth off the table and dashed out again without giving any explanation and apparently without noticing the damage to the house.

We crouched under the table not knowing what to do until police and wardens came to help us out and escort us across to the Anderson shelter, already crowded with neighbours, including several small children. We sat on upright dining chairs so close together that our feet almost touched in the circle we made, about a dozen adults, not counting children, with only a small nightlight to give a glimmer of light. I sat there all night with my dog on my lap, listening to the noise from outside and wondering what was happening out there, occasionally dozing off with my head resting on the dog.

In the morning we came out of the shelter to find that two landmines had fallen in our short road, causing a great deal of damage. Our home could be used, although we couldn't get upstairs, and doors, windows and some ceilings were missing, as well as some furniture and possessions damaged.

One mine had fallen in a small wooded area so the blast had been slightly diverted, but the other had landed directly on the home of a young couple with three little boys. They had been on their way home after doing some shopping and were the people I had heard speak to my father the night before. The mine went off as they walked up their garden path and the whole family were killed except for the six-month-old baby, who was found alive in his dead mother's arms. The tablecloth my father took out of our house was used to cover the remains of the two little boys after Dad had collected them together, as they'd been blown to pieces.[21]

The idea of bombing enemy civilian populations was adopted by the Allies. In February 1942, the British Deputy Chief of the Air Staff wrote to Sir Arthur Harris, the head of the RAF Bomber Command.

. . . it has been decided that the primary object of your operations should now be focused on the morale of the enemy civil population and, in particular, industrial workers.

Sir Arthur Harris seemed to think this was a good idea.

We are going to scourge the Third Reich from end to end. We are bombing Germany city by city and ever more terribly in order to make it impossible for her to go on with the war. That is our object, and we shall pursue it relentlessly.[22]

The Allies began bombing German cities in March 1942. R Andreas-Friedrich wrote in his diary about life in Berlin during the bombing of winter 1943–4.

Why do millions of people keep on trying to build up what in the next few hours may lie in ruins?

I observe the faces of the sweepers and the men who board up the windows. I look at my own face in the mirror. Crusted with dirt, my head-scarf slips down askew across my forehead. And I believe I have found the answer. We repair things and rebuild because we have to. When our living-room is destroyed we move into the kitchen.

When the kitchen is broken up we move out into the corridor. When the corridor is reduced to rubble we set up home in the cellar. If only we are able to keep our homes. The paltriest corner of home is better than any palace far away . . . You can't go on living if you don't belong anywhere. That's why the first thing people rescue from their burning homes is their pillow, because it is a last piece of 'home'.

Neither sweeping away rubble, nor rescuing pillows has got anything to do with sympathy for Nazism. Nobody thinks of Hitler when he boards up his kitchen window. But everyone does think of the fact that you cannot survive in the cold and that before evening comes and the sirens wail you must have a refuge where you can stretch out your limbs.[23]

In a visit to the USA in May 1943, Churchill referred to the need to bomb Japan. He spoke of:

. . . the process, so necessary and desirable, of laying the cities and other munitions centres of Japan in ashes, for in ashes they must surely lie before peace comes back to the world.[24]

When entire Japanese cities were being bombed in 1944, Gwen Terasaki, the American wife of a Japanese diplomat, was offered a small house in the hills as a refuge for her family. Their problem, all too soon, was hunger.

The only vegetable that seemed to thrive on our mountain ledge was the turnip. We ate not only the turnip but the leafy top. The Japanese are very fond of simply-cooked greens and, having no supplies, I could cook only in their manner. They wash them and cook them in a pot with the lid fastened tightly, using only the water that clings to the leaves. Afterwards the vegetable is cooled, drained, chopped into intricate shapes, and usually garnished with shredded bonito. We saved our butter for breakfast and there was never enough *shōyu* sauce for seasoning.

The three of us were growing much weaker. I had lost my physical energy and suffered from a mental lethargy which made me very forgetful. When one starves slowly, it is not a spectacular thing, a great yearning for food and craving to eat. One is content to sit in the sun and do nothing; one even forgets that there is anything to do. One loses control of tears and lets them roll unheeded down one's cheek. It took me at least forty minutes to an hour every morning to comb my hair. My arms ached if I kept them up to my head for more than a minute or so. I had to stop and rest several times before I was finished. Mako's hair was another chore. Her long pigtails reached almost to her waist, and, since she could not do them herself and I was unable to do them for her, we finally had to cut them off.[25]

As the bombing of Japan grew more fierce and concentrated, it became 'fire-bombing', the deliberate creation of tornado-like winds of fire that engulfed thousands of people. A French journalist, Robert Guillain, saw what happened in Tokyo on the night of 29 November 1944.

In the rare places where the fire hoses are functioning (for water is scarce or pressureless in most of the canal areas) the firemen hose down the refugees so that they may safely escape through fiery passages. Elsewhere, people douse themselves in the trough that sits in front of each house before continuing their flight. But the flight is an obstacle course: the electric poles and wires which spin a thick web around Tokyo have fallen across the road. In the thick smoke, with a wind so fiery that it burns the lungs, the fugitives collapse before burning up in place. The wind beats the flaming currents to the ground and often it is the feet that catch fire first: the leggings of the men and the trousers of the women ignite and the rest follows suit. The air-raid clothing distributed by the government consists of thickly padded hoods which cover the head and shoulders. These hoods are especially designed to protect the ears from the noise of explosives – for Tokyo has been under bomb attack for many months. The hoods ignite under the downpour of sparks, and those whose feet do not catch fire burn first at their heads. Mothers, carrying babies strapped to their backs in the Japanese style, suddenly notice (often too late) that their infants' blankets have caught fire. [26]

In England, in February 1944, Bishop Bell of Chichester had protested in the House of Lords that such indiscriminate bombing was not legitimate according to international law.

I desire to challenge the Government on the policy which directs the bombing of enemy towns on the present scale, especially with reference to civilians, non-combatants, and non-military and non-industrial objectives . . .

The point I want to bring home, because I doubt whether it is sufficiently realized, is that it is no longer definite military and industrial objectives which are the aim of the bombers, but the whole town, area by area, is plotted carefully out. This area is singled out and plastered on one night; that area is singled out and plastered on another night; a third, a fourth, a fifth area is similarly singled out and plastered night after night, till, to use the language of the Chief of Bomber Command with regard to Berlin, the heart of Nazi Germany ceases to beat. How can there be discrimination in such matters when civilians, monuments, military objectives and industrial objectives all together form the target? How can the bombers aim at anything more than a great space when they see nothing and the bombing is blind? [27]

D Hornsey, an English bomber-pilot, homeward-bound, had his own misgivings.

I was pleased in one way to learn our raid had been so successful, but my heart sank very low in my boots when I thought of the cost involved. Nor, on sober reflection, was I able to think without a pang, of the number of civilians who must have been killed, for they must have included many women and children. I was thankful that the target selected was not my responsibility . . . No doubt the fact that the target was an industrial area . . . justified the raid in the eyes of the authorities. It was not for me to question policy, nor could it have made any difference (except to me) if I had done so.[28]

And so did a German pilot, P W Stahl.

On the flight back across the North Sea I thought about the sense and purpose of air-raids. Although I can rely on Hans completely that he does everything he can to find important military targets for our bombs, I know at the same time how possible it is that we might drop our bombs on places where they have no effect. But what if we hit a residential area or a hospital? This is a cruel war! But the other side has the same problem too. I wonder how many Britons are thinking the same as me?[29]

Leningrad in Russia was not heavily bombed during the war, but it was under siege by the Germans in 1942, which caused great hardship. An American historian wrote:

There was hardly a cat or a dog left in Leningrad by late December. They had all been eaten. But the trauma was great when a man came to butcher an animal which had lived on his affection for years. One elderly artist strangled his pet cat and ate it, according to Vsevolod Vishnevsky. Later, he tried to hang himself, but the rope failed, he fell to the floor, breaking his leg, and froze to death. The smallest Leningrad children grew up not knowing what cats and dogs were. One of the most savage attacks directed at Anna Akhmatova in the postwar years was written by a Leningrad working girl who accused the great poetess of ignorance of Leningrad in the blockade years because, in a poem, she spoke of pigeons in the square before the Kazan Cathedral. There were no pigeons there, the girl asserted. They all had long since been eaten.[30]

WOMEN IN THE WAR

In the grey light of morning, nurses' bodies were found covering young children. They had died that others might live.

Revd A P Wales, hospital chaplain, England [31]

Women in the national armies, navies and air forces of the Second World War did not drive tanks, fly on bombing raids, or go to sea in submarines. There were no women generals, and no women prime ministers, emperors, *duces* or presidents either. But women fought with weapons in many resistance movements, and did everything else that men did, including die in great numbers. Lettice Curtis flew planes around Britain, not in battle, but because they had to be moved around the country.

Nobody had really allowed for this task of moving aircraft from the factories. The RAF thought they could do it themselves, but of course they couldn't . . . When the time came they were desperately short of RAF pilots. And when the factories built up they were short of pilots of any shape or size that could move an aircraft. It was so acute they didn't mind if you were a man, woman or monkey. Nobody had allowed for the vast number of planes coming out of the factories, and the amount of work it would involve. We had to move them as soon as they were ready, so the factories didn't get gummed up. You took them to an RAF maintenance unit and they were delivered to the RAF.

And then later we took them to the squadrons as soon as they were ready.

There was some opposition to women pilots to start with. People wrote in to the *Aeroplane* saying how wicked and contemptible it all was to employ them. The editor of the magazine wrote about women being a menace thinking they could cope with piloting a high-speed bomber, when some of them weren't intelligent enough to scrub a hospital floor decently. But I personally didn't come across any prejudice against women. We were soon treated equally and there was very little bias against us; eventually we got equal pay with men. After all, when there's a war on, you get on with your job; I don't think you look over your shoulder and criticize what anyone else is doing. You hadn't time when you were doing a job of national importance.[32]

Galina Vishnevskaya, in peacetime a famous Russian opera singer, had a much less glamorous job in wartime Kronstadt.

Our duty was to keep round-the-clock watch from the towers; we had to report to headquarters the location of any flares or fires we spotted; or, in case of a bombing or artillery fire, where the explosions were, and what part of the town was being attacked. Immediately after an air-raid alert sounded, we had to be ready to help the civilian population: to dig people out of the rubble of buildings destroyed by explosion, to minister first aid, and so on. During the day we were involved in cleaning up the town. We tore down wooden buildings for fuel and issued firewood to the population. (The same thing was done in Leningrad, where not a single wooden building was left standing.)

We had no equipment to speak of except our hands, crowbars, and shovels. During the severe winter, sewage pipes had ruptured everywhere; and as soon as the ground thawed out, the sewage system had to be repaired. The women of the 'blue division' took care of it. We did it in a very simple way. Suppose there was a street 1,000 metres long. First we would use crowbars to pry up the cobblestones and would remove them with our hands. Then we would dig up the earth out of a trench some two metres deep with shovels. In the trench there would be wooden planking covering the pipe. We would pry up the planks with crowbars and repair the part of the pipe that had ruptured. The recipe was as simple and clear as in a cookbook. In the process, I even learned how a sewage system is built. Of course I had to stand in filth up to my knees, but that didn't matter – I was being fed![33]

From August 1941, the young women and men of Leningrad had to help fortify the city against the invading German armies.

Youngsters from the universities and institutes were corraled into the fortifications tasks. Unlike the ordinary Leningraders, who were drafted without pay, the youngsters got nine roubles a day – more than their scholarship allowances.

One morning Bychevsky got a telephone call from his oldest daughter, a first-year student at Leningrad University.

'Good-bye, Papa,' the youngster said, 'I'm off to work.'

'Where?'

'You know where, I think. We're going in a car. I have to hurry.'

'What are you taking with you?'

'What do I need?' the girl replied. 'A towel. Some soap. I don't need anything else.'

'Wait a minute,' her father said. 'Wait a minute, young lady. Have you got a coat, a kettle, a spoon or a knapsack? And you must take some bread, some sugar, some linen.'

'You're joking, Papa,' the girl replied gaily. 'None of the girls is taking anything. We won't be gone long. We'll sleep in a haystack. Tell Mama not to worry. See you soon.'

But, as Bychevsky noted, the girls did not return so quickly. Nor did all return. They came back, not by car, but on foot, weary to exhaustion, their clothes in rags, their bodies aching, their hands raw, their feet bruised, black with dirt and heavy with sweat. Many bore bloody bandages over their wounds. Some were buried (and some were not) in the open fields and beside the roads, where they were caught by flights of low-flying JU-88s and Heinkel attack bombers. The planes flew over, day after day, bombing and strafing. How many thousands were killed? No one knows. There was no accurate count of those engaged on the job and no way of identifying who returned and who did not.[34]

Lieutenant Juanita Redmond served in the US Army Nurse Corps on Bataan in the Philippines in 1942. The Americans were fighting the Japanese who had occupied the Philippines (see page 46). In her book, published in 1943, she described how the men coped with the consequences of injury.

One youngster from Texas whose arm had been amputated worried a great deal about his girl. If he ever got home – that was the familiar phrase – they were going to be married. At least, that was what they had planned. Now, he didn't know. Maybe he shouldn't with only one arm. Maybe she wouldn't want him. At that point we would always hurry to tell him how proud the girl would be of him and of course they would get married, it would be plain foolishness not to. Only the other boys who had had amputations remained silent.[35]

But she also found some humour in their worsening situation.

At Limay we had been lucky enough to have a Filipino civilian do our laundry, which he did very nicely, taking the greatest pains with our white uniforms. However, later on our clothes were left unpressed, and attached to each girl's bundle was a note:

> *'Dear mum, I am sorry to return your clothes no finish press but we cannot get charcoal. As we are at war, I know you will understand and will not mind wearing your clothes unpress from top to bottom. I am your faithful servant until the Japs come get me.'* [36]

Joanne Stavridi was a nurse in Crete during the Nazi assault there in May 1941. For her, it was men who were really responsible for wars.

If this war has done nothing else it's made me a much more ardent feminist than ever before. We women have had to sit by and watch all we cared for and loved smashed to smithereens and haven't been allowed a say in the matter. I trust and hope that we shall rise up in a battalion when it's over and insist on having an equal say in the future arrangements of the world, so that we may stop men making fools of themselves and wrecking our homes and killing our husbands and children. [37]

IN THE PACIFIC

By early 1941, American troops in the Philippines were keeping a sharp eye open for ominous signs of a coming attack. Abie Abrahams, who was one of them, later recounted this episode in his book.

We knew that Japan was going to strike somewhere. The 31st Infantry went on alert in July, 1941. We placed men on the tallest buildings with radio and compass to report any plane activities.

Japanese fishing increased heavily. Thousands came as fishermen. This was a real joke to us.

The 31st Infantry was ordered to Corregidor for beach and target firing. The Battalion Commander assigned me to be in charge of repairing targets that were pulled by a small boat. Our boat was to pull four targets. When the targets were inside the buoy our regiment were to fire when I raised the white flag. Our boat moved toward the buoy.

'Sergeant Abrahams, look!' one of the men yelled.

I took the field glasses and focused over the horizon. Two small fishing crafts met my eyes.

'Raise the red flag,' I said.

'What's the trouble, Sergeant?' the Colonel asked, thinking perhaps, that a cable had broken.

'Sir, there are two small fishing crafts in the area.'

'Proceed and investigate.'

When we arrived alongside the small boats, six slant-eyes stared back at me from under large straw hats.

'Don't you people know you're in a restricted area?' I asked.

They gave me a sheepish look, grinned, then turned their crafts away.

An hour later they were back.

'They're back,' I told the Colonel as I raised the red flag.

'Raise the white flag,' he ordered.

When the 31st Infantry saw the white flag hell broke loose from the beach. Machine-gun and rifles hit the targets.

The Japanese fishermen, who were spying on us, lost no time in moving out as rapidly as their crafts could go.[38]

Slant-eyes A derogatory expression used to describe the Japanese.

In a space of hours on 7 and 8 December, 1941, the Japanese attacked Siam (now Thailand), Hong Kong, Malaya – and Pearl Harbor. Admiral Stark, Chief of Naval Operations in Washington, had forecast what would happen. He had written to Admiral Kimmel, Pearl Harbor, on 24 November.

Top Secret

Chances of favourable outcome of negotiations with Japan very doubtful. This situation coupled with statements of Japanese Government and movements of their naval and military forces indicate in our opinion that a surprise aggressive movement in any direction including attack on Philippines or Guam is a possibility. Utmost secrecy necessary in order not to complicate an already tense situation or precipitate Japanese action.[39]

Guam An island in the North Pacific where US bases were situated.

The Japanese attack on Pearl Harbor brought the United States into the war. The Philippine Islands were also bombed by Japan. American troops fought furiously there, on the peninsula of Bataan, but the Japanese took control in April 1942. Abie Abrahams was imprisoned in a Japanese work camp. Many years later he went back to Bataan, and remembered the horror of that time.

I gazed out at the mighty mountains of Bataan standing lofty in the bright moonlight. I saw them guarding the piles of empty beer bottles from which the enemy drank while American and Filipino prisoners fell to the ground from thirst. I saw again the piles of yellowed cigarette butts, and cans from which they ate while their prisoners collapsed and died from hunger and starvation. The hollow faces of my friends, all heroes of Bataan, who were buried on the hot plains with metal identification tags attached to the broken crosses. The barbed wire fences enclosing the prisons appeared on the horizon of my memory. They were isolated far out on the grass-covered uncultivated western Tarlac plains, a few miles from the purple range of the Zambales Mountains that surrounded the village of Cabu. Inside these enclosures I see the sick men, too weak to cry, and the dying. I see their sunken eyes and shallow cheeks. The haggard men marching in a long, long line, along the agonizing miles of the Bataan *Death March*, most of whom never returned. The roar of large guns echoes through my head, and bombs exploding, and trampling, staggering, plodding sounds of sore and bleeding feet die with the distance. Suffering victims cry in loud voices, 'Help me, God.'[40]

Bataan **Death March** *The long march to the Japanese work camps, during which many prisoners died.*

Some Americans hid and stayed on in the Philippines after April 1942, working with the Filipinos in a resistance group against the Japanese. Louise Reed Spencer and her husband were among them. She recalled celebrating Thanksgiving in the mountains with friends, while the war continued all around them.

That Thanksgiving dinner was something to remember. The turkey, perfectly browned and succulent, was stuffed with rice seasoned with some prepared dressing Laura had found and saved among her canned goods. With it were giblet gravy thickened with saba flour, mashed camotes (yams), mashed squash, a can of peas and carrots, a can of cranberry sauce, and the last of our bottled pickles. For dessert we had a sort of Indian Pudding, the recipe of which Laura made up herself. It contained the last of the dates and nuts the Roses had brought to the hills, and served with it was canned cream, the last of a few treasured cans. There was native coffee to finish off with, not quite American coffee – but good, mind you, good!

As the crowning glory of this feast, we had two bottles of wine which the Fords sent over with their greetings. We chilled it by setting it in the creek for a little while before serving. Having it added the final festive touch. Mr and Mrs Rose refused to take even a sip, for they were total abstainers, but they very kindly loaned us their communion cups to drink it from. They said wine from our terrible old tin cups would be unthinkable. They had brought glasses up to the hills for the monthly communion services, but the supply of grape juice was gone now and no more communion services could be held.

It was a beautiful Thanksgiving party, and we all felt rather as the pilgrims themselves might have felt when they had come through their first hard year. We had spent nearly a year – for Pearl Harbor was almost a year ago – in a state of alarm and flight from the Japs, and during the latter half of that time had been living more primitively than we had ever imagined. Actually, the hardships we had suffered didn't amount to much, but at that time they still looked fairly great in comparison with our normal lives. We were deeply thankful to have come through to another Thanksgiving, and we ended our party by singing, all together, 'Praise God From Whom All Blessings Flow' and 'God Bless America'.

The harsh realities of our existence were brought home to us that night, when we heard the sound of shelling off in the direction of the highway.[41]

The Japanese had quickly overrun Malaya and the Philippines. It was not just brilliant planning, according to the Japanese colonel, Masonubu Tsuji.

Mr Churchill, in his memoirs, implies that the Japanese Army before the outbreak of hostilities made secret preparations in each Malay district for comprehensive aggression – even, he says, to the storage of bicycles. With regret I have to say that these are not the facts of the case. The truth is that Japanese-manufactured bicycles, because of their cheapness, had become one of the chief exports from Japan to the whole of South-east Asia, where they were widely purchased by the inhabitants. For this reason replacements and spare parts were easily available everywhere throughout Malaya. When viewed from this angle, the incorrect observation of an Englishman, even one in Mr Churchill's position, can scarcely meet with approval.

The greatest difficulty encountered in the use of bicycles was the excessive heat, owing to which the tyres punctured easily. A bicycle repair squad of at least two men was attached to every company, and each squad repaired an average of about twenty machines a day. But such repairs were only makeshift. When the enemy were being hotly pursued, and time was pressing, punctured tyres were taken off and the bicycles ridden on the rims. Surprisingly enough they ran smoothly on the paved roads, which were in perfect condition. Numbers of bicycles, some with tyres and some without, when passing along the road, made a noise resembling that of tanks. At night when such bicycle units advanced the enemy frequently retreated hurriedly, saying, 'Here come the tanks!' 'It is the tanks, it is the tanks!'

When in trouble our troops would dive into the jungle carrying their bicycles on their shoulders. The difficulties of trying to break through jungle carrying their arms and with bicycles on their shoulders can well be imagined.

Even the long-legged Englishmen could not escape our troops on bicycles. This was the reason why they were continually driven off the road into the jungle, where, with their retreat cut off, they were forced to surrender.

Thanks to Britain's dear money spent on the excellent paved roads, and to the cheap Japanese bicycles, the assault on Malaya was easy.[42]

The Japanese were set to invade Australia, until in October 1942 Australian and American troops finally stopped them at the island of Guadalcanal, the largest of the Solomon Islands. For two years, they pushed the Japanese back northwards from island to island. The US general, Robert Eichelberger, recalled in his book how his troops disliked the jungle.

Actually, this long after, I'm inclined to believe that the men were more frightened by the jungle than by the Japanese. It was the terror of the new and the unknown. There is nothing pleasant about sinking into a foul-smelling bog up to your knees. There is nothing pleasant about lying in a slit trench, half submerged, while a tropical rain turns it into a river. Jungle night noises were strange to Americans – and in the moist hot darkness the rustling of small animals in the bush was easily misinterpreted as the stealthy approach of the enemy. I can recall one night hearing a noise that sounded like a man brushing against my tent. It turned out that a leaf had fallen from a tree and struck the canvas side. The stem of the leaf was as thick as my thumb. It measured two and a half feet long by one and a half feet wide.[43]

At the beginning of the conflict with the USA, this Japanese soldier thought the American troops inexperienced in jungle warfare.

The enemy has received almost no training. Even though we fire a shot they present a very large portion of their body and look around. Their movements are very slow. At this rate they cannot make a night attack.

They hit coconuts that are fifteen metres from us. There are some low shots but most of them are high. They do not look out and determine their targets from the jungle. They are in the jungle firing as long as their ammunition lasts. Maybe they get more money for firing so many rounds.[44]

But by 1944, as this soldier's diary shows, it was the Japanese who felt menaced by the jungle.

22 April 1944: Resigned to death, I entered the muddy jungle. Enemy airplanes are flying overhead. I am hungry and am beginning to become alarmed about the situation. I plunged through the jungle because I believe it is dangerous to remain here. The vast expanse of the jungle cannot be expressed in words.

2 May 1944: At a small creek. There is no end to this life. We are still roaming aimlessly on the thirteenth day. Perhaps this is part of our fate. We hoped that we would meet our commander and his amiable staff. We are beginning to hate everything in this world. We live each day sympathizing with one another. At times, we see someone in our group shedding tears.

24 May 1944: . . . The jungle is everywhere, and there is absolutely no water in this area. We must reach Kotabaru or we will all die.

26 May 1944: In the wilderness. As we proceeded farther we met our troops. This force was retreating from Aitape. They were shouldering rice which they stole from Kotabaru supply depot. I heard the news from the commanding officer. It was terrifying news. They had marched ahead with the men falling dead one by one.[45]

Not everyone in Japan had wanted war. An anonymous Japanese farmer grumbled about his son going to war.

If only Osamu had not been drafted I could have gotten by without help from others. But look at the fix I'm in. They didn't give any advance notice. Suddenly there was a draft notice and he was gone. Just like a cat dragged off by the scruff of its neck. Now I'm stuck since he left. No matter how many other countries we occupy or how many victories we win, it doesn't add one inch to my paddy fields. Talk about something that doesn't pay. There's nothing as stupid as war.[46]

Near the end of the war, anti-war feeling in Japan was strong. The Police Bureau Report of August 1945 quoted those who were resentful of the authorities.

Government officials and the military just keep shouting encouragement while they allow the populace to be slaughtered. The people are being killed off by the thousands every day. Yet the nation's leaders don't seem at all troubled by the death and destruction. Do they think of us as human beings? What are we to them, just cannon fodder? I never realized till this war what a vicious, ruthless country Japan is.

The Emperor looks very carefree in his photograph. He's killed off a million mothers' sons and he sits there looking unconcerned.[47]

Emperor Emperor Hirohito

ENDINGS

For Hitler and the Nazis, the beginning of the end was the plot to kill Hitler. In July 1944, some high-ranking German officers, convinced that Hitler was leading their country to disaster, tried to assassinate him. Hitler survived their bomb, and the very same day he and some of his military officers and important officials met the Italian dictator, Benito Mussolini. An American diplomat, Allen Dulles, tells the story of that 'mad tea party'. This account was probably written using information from a book by Hitler's interpreter.

They were not a gay party. Hitler, still white [from the shock of the assassination attempt], told Mussolini he had just had the greatest piece of luck in his life. Together they inspected the mass of debris at the scene of the explosion. At five o'clock they started their conference. The Führer was silent and for a long time sat gazing into space, munching. the vari-coloured pills supplied him by Professor Theo Morell, the quack he made his physician. But the others, more or less ignoring their Italian visitors, began to quarrel, and to blame one another because the war had not yet been won. Ribbentrop raged against the generals and insisted on being called *von* Ribbentrop. (Only adoption in 1925 by his spinster aunt, Gertrud, had given him the right to use *von*.) Göring threatened him with his marshal's baton. Keitel tried to make excuses. Mussolini was aghast, and tried to maintain his dignity among the barbarians of the north . . .

At this point someone telephoned from Berlin to say that order had not yet been restored there. Hitler took the telephone himself and again began to shriek. He gave the SS in Berlin full power to shoot anyone they wished and completely lost his temper when he heard that Himmler, who had only just left East Prussia to take over in Berlin, had not yet arrived there.

Then Hitler calmed down, and started a monologue of self-pity. The German people, he said, were unworthy of his greatness, and no one appreciated what he had done for them. This elicited emphatic denials from his henchmen, who vied with one another to convince the Führer of their loyalty. Göring recounted what he had done for the Nazi cause and the Air Force. Doenitz extolled the heroism of the Navy. But then Göring and Ribbentrop started quarrelling again. And so it went until the SS officer led the bewildered Italian visitors away.

While this mad tea party went on in East Prussia, in the rest of Germany the blood purge began. Thousands were rounded up, arrested, tortured and killed in order that Hitler's Thousand-Year Reich might survive another two hundred and ninety days.[48]

Thousand-Year Reich *Hitler had declared in his writings that the Third Reich would rule for a thousand years.*

Von *The prefix to the surname of a German aristocrat.*

A German prisoner of war, who asked his interviewer not to name him, ended the war in an American POW camp at Rheinsberg, eastern Germany.

19 May 1945: If I ever survive this camp, I will collect poems under the title Comfort and Praise. Today I got four potatoes. What riches!

20 May 1945: How long will we have to be without shelter, without blankets or tents? Every German soldier once had shelter from the weather. Even a dog has a doghouse to crawl into when it rains. Our only wish is finally after six weeks to get a roof over our heads. Even a savage is better housed. Diogenes, Diogenes, you at least had your barrel.

22 May 1945: The story of the cardboard. Our rations come into the camp in large cardboard cartons. Broken apart, these can serve as a kind of bed. The cardboard, about one metre 20 centimetres long and body-width, provides good insulation against the damp ground. Every day about 25 such 'beds' are given out by the doctor to those who can prove they have no tent, blanket or coat. Properly speaking,

I was not really entitled to one because I still had a coat. At about eight o'clock on the morning of the first day that I tried to get one, there were over 25 men in line before me. Next morning I got up about 6.30, before reveille. Lucky me! I had my cardboard. Profoundly happy, I clutched it under my arm and lugged it to my hole. From then on it was my prize possession. We are hand in glove together.[49]

Diogenes *A Greek philosopher who was said to have lived such a simple life that he spent his time in a tub.*

The war in the Pacific ended after the USA dropped two atom bombs on Japan in August 1945. But before that, Japan's situation had become hopeless. Fears that the Americans would soon invade had led to suggestions about a kind of home guard defence. Gwen Terasaki recalled a meeting in her village.

The *kumicho* called the meeting to order. There were two main items on the agenda. First, every person of adult age must provide himself with a bamboo spear of a certain length with which to meet the enemy when they came to the islands. I was so shocked by this I sat in stunned silence . . . They began to argue over the length of the spears . . .[50]

Kumicho *Village leader.*

The first atom bomb was dropped on Hiroshima on 6 August, the second on Nagasaki three days later. A Japanese journalist described the effects of the Hiroshima bomb.

At nine minutes past seven in the morning an air-raid warning sounded and four American B-29 planes appeared. To the north of the town two of them turned and made off to the south and disappeared in the direction of the Shoho Sea. The other two, after having circled the neighbourhood of Shukai, flew off at high speed southwards in the direction of the Bingo Sea.

At 7.31 the all-clear was given. Feeling themselves in safety, people came out of their shelters and went about their affairs and the work of the day began.

Suddenly a glaring whitish pinkish light appeared in the sky accompanied by an unnatural tremor which was followed almost immediately by a wave of suffocating heat and a wind which swept away everything in its path.

Within a few seconds the thousands of people in the streets and the gardens in the centre of the town were scorched by a wave of searing heat. Many were killed instantly, others lay writhing on the ground screaming in agony from the intolerable pain of their burns.

Everything standing upright in the way of the blast – walls, houses, factories and other buildings – was annihilated and the debris spun round in a whirlwind and was carried up into the air. Trams were picked up and tossed aside as though they had neither weight nor solidity. Trains were flung off the rails as though they were toys. Horses, dogs and cattle suffered the same fate as human beings. Every living thing was petrified in an attitude of indescribable suffering. Even the vegetation did not escape. Trees went up in flames, the rice plants lost their greenness, the grass burned on the ground like dry straw.

Beyond the zone of utter death in which nothing remained alive houses collapsed in a whirl of beams, bricks and girders. Up to about three miles from the centre of the explosion lightly-built houses were flattened as though they had been built of cardboard. Those who were inside were either killed or wounded. Those who managed to extricate themselves by some miracle found themselves surrounded by a ring of fire. And the few who succeeded in making their way to safety generally died twenty or thirty days later from the delayed effects of the deadly gamma-rays. Some of the reinforced concrete or stone buildings remained standing, but their interiors were completely gutted by the blast.

About half an hour after the explosion, whilst the sky all around Hiroshima was still cloudless, a fine rain began to fall on the town and went on for about five minutes. It was caused by the sudden rise of over-heated air to a great height, where it condensed and fell back as rain. Then a violent wind rose and the fires extended with terrible rapidity, because most Japanese houses are built only of timber and straw.

By the evening the fire began to die down and then it went out. There was nothing left to burn. Hiroshima had ceased to exist.[51]

Later, for the first time since the war began, Emperor Hirohito went visiting amongst the people.

Immense crowds choked the line of travel as they went by car through the villages and towns and cities of Japan. The people would surge towards the car, cheering, tearful in their joy to look upon the *tennō* [Emperor]. An old lady held up the photo of her lost son for the Emperor to look at, saying, 'Look upon him, look upon him, I beg you. He died for you!'[52]

Important Dates

1933

30 Jan Hitler comes to power in Germany.

1939

Mar German troops occupy Czechoslovakia.

Aug German–Soviet Pact.

1 Sep German troops occupy Poland.

2 Sep France and Britain declare war against Germany.

1940

Apr Germany invades Denmark and Norway.

May German army attacks Western Europe, invading France, Holland, Belgium and Luxembourg.

10 Jun Italy declares war on France and Britain.

22 Jun France signs an armistice with the Third Reich.

Aug Japan, Italy and Germany sign the Tripartite (Axis) Pact.

Aug–Oct Germany bombs English towns in the Battle of Britain.

Oct Italy attacks Greece.

Nov Greece drives the Italians out.

1941

Jan–May Germany takes over Romania, Bulgaria, Yugoslavia, Greece and Crete.

Apr USSR signs a neutrality pact with Japan.

22 Jun Germany attacks the USSR.

30 Aug Beginning of the 900-day siege of Leningrad, Russia, by the Germans.

7 Dec Japan attacks the US base of Pearl Harbor in the Hawaiian Islands.

11 Dec Germany and Italy declare war on the USA. The USA enters the war on the side of Britain and the USSR.

1942

Jan–May Japanese conquests in the Pacific, including Malaya, Singapore and the Philippines.

Mar Allies begin bombing German cities.

Apr Bombing of Tokyo, Japan by the Allies.

Jun The Allied forces begin to fight the Japanese in the Pacific.

4–7 Jun US air and sea victory in the battle at Midway (a small area of land in the middle of the Pacific, with strategic significance).

Oct US and Australian troops defeat the Japanese at the island of Guadalcanal, the largest of the Solomon Islands.

British forces defeat the Germans at the battle of El Alamein in Egypt.

8 Nov Allied landing in North Africa.

1943

Jan Defeat of the German army in Stalingrad.

Warsaw ghetto uprising begins.

Jul USSR defeats German army at the battle of Kursk.

9 Jul Allies land in Sicily.

3 Sep Italy signs an armistice with the Allies.

13 Oct Italy declares war on Germany.

1944

Jun–Oct Allies defeat Germans in France and Belgium.

6 Jun Allied landings in Normandy, France – D-Day.

22 Jun The USSR launches an attack on the Germans from the east.

Jul Some high-ranking German officers attempt to assassinate Hitler.

15 Aug Allies land in the south of France and defeat the Germans.

25 Aug US landings in the Philippines.

1945

4–11 Feb British, US and Soviet leaders meet at the Yalta Conference.

Mar Allies cross the Rhine and break through German lines.

30 Apr Hitler commits suicide.

8 May Germany surrenders.

6 Aug Atomic bomb dropped on Hiroshima.

9 Aug Atomic bomb dropped on Nagasaki.

15 Aug Japan surrenders.

Glossary

Aliens   The name given to foreigners living in Britain.
Allied soldiers   Soldiers of the Allied armies that fought against Germany, Japan and Italy.
Bren carrier   The carrier for Bren guns, which were gas-operated light machine-guns used by the British Army.
Concentration camps   Guarded camps in which prisoners are held.
Exemplary   A model, fit for imitation.
Feminist   Someone who believes in equal rights for women.
Interned   Imprisoned.
Kultur   The German word for civilization.
Luftwaffe   The German Air Force.
Paratrooper   A soldier who is trained and equipped to be dropped by parachute into a battle area.
POW   Prisoner of war.
Reveille   A signal, usually given by a bugle or drum, to awaken soldiers or sailors in the morning.
RAF   Royal Air Force (Britain).
SS   The organization within the Nazi party that provided Hitler's security forces and concentration camp guards.
Third Reich   The name of Hitler's regime, meaning Third Empire.
Tracer   Ammunition that can be observed when in flight by the burning of chemical substances in it.

Further reading

My Childhood in Nazi Germany by Elsbeth Emmerich with Robert Hull (Wayland, 1991)
The Diary of Anne Frank by Anne Frank (Pan Books, 1968)
The Home Front series by Fiona Reynoldson (Wayland, 1990–91)
King's Men by Tom McCarthy (Pluto Press, 1990)
Poetry of the Second World War, selected by Edward Hudson (Wayland, 1990)
World War II, America at War series (Facts on File Publications, 1992)

Notes on Sources

1 Cited in Guy Chapman, *Vain Glory*, p.734, Cassell, London, 1937.

2 Cited in *ibid.*, p.734.

3 Marie-Christine Gouin, cited in Patricia Williams (ed.), *Children at War*, p.29, BBC, London, 1989.

4 Cited in Philip Hallie, *Lest Innocent Blood be Shed*, p.103, Michael Joseph, London, 1979.

5 Ben Helfgott, cited in Anton Gill, *The Journey Back from Hell*, Grafton Books, London, 1988.

6 Alexander Donat, *Holocaust Kingdom*, p.255, Holocaust Library, New York, 1963.

7 Jewish Armed Resistance Organization, cited in *The Ghetto Fights* by Marek Edelman, Bookmarks, London, 1990; from the Polish edition, Warsaw, 1945.

8 Cited in Desmond Flower and James Reeves, *The War, 1939–45*, p.400; from *Six Against Tyranny*, Inger Schmoll, Murray, London, 1955.

9 T R Latham, minute of meeting in Foreign Office (Refugee Committee) cited in Bernard Wasserstein, *Britain and the Jews of Europe, 1939–45*, p.109, Institute of Jewish Affairs, Oxford University Press, 1979.

10 Proceedings at Nuremberg, Trial of Major German War Criminals, HMSO, 1946, cited in Flower and Reeves, *op. cit.*, p.830.

11 Cited in Flower and Reeves, *op. cit.*, p.91; from Milton Shulman, *Defeat in the West*, Secker and Warburg, London, 1947.

12 Pascal Jardin, *Vichy Boyhood*, p.36, Faber & Faber, London.

13 Guy Remington, cited in *New Yorker Book of War Pieces*, p.339, Bloomsbury, London, 1989.

14 R M Wingfield, *Only Way Out*, Hutchinson, London, 1955, cited in Flower and Reeves, *op. cit.*, p.916.

15 Walter Bernstein, cited in *New Yorker Book of War Pieces, op. cit.*, p.242.

16 Cited in Barry Turner, *And the Policeman Smiled*, p.98, Bloomsbury, London, 1990.

17 *Ibid.*, p.58.

18 *Ibid.*, p.144.

19 Cited in Wasserstein, *op. cit.*, p.96.

20 Turner, *op. cit.*, p.152.

21 Dorothy Barton, cited in Tom Harrison, *Living Through the Blitz*, p.18, Penguin Books, London, 1990.

22 Sir Arthur Harris, cited in *Earthquake Hour*, ed. Caws and Watts, Blackie, London, 1975.

23 R Andreas-Friedrich, cited in Peter Dines and Peter Knoch, *People in the Bombing War*, p.37; from *Schauplatz Berlin: Ein Deutsches Tagesbuch (1938–48)*, Lentz, Berlin, 1962.

24 Winston Churchill, cited in John W Dower, *War Without Mercy*, p.55, Pantheon Books, New York, 1986; from Christopher Thorne, *Allies of a Kind*, Oxford University Press, 1978.

25 Gwen Terasaki, cited in Livingston, Moore and Oldfather, *The Japan Reader, Vol. I*, p.469, Penguin, 1973; from Terasaki, *Bridge to the Sun*, Michael Joseph, 1958.

26 Robert Guillain, cited in *ibid.*, p.475; from Guillain, *Le Peuple Japonais et la Guerre*, p.198, Réné Juillard, Paris, 1947.

27 Bishop Bell, speech in House of Lords, 9 February 1944.

28 D Hornsey, cited in Dines and Knoch, *op. cit.*, p.37; from *Here Today Bomb Tomorrow, Book 2*, papers in Imperial War Museum, London.

29 P W Stahl, cited in *ibid.*, p.37; from *Kampfflieger zwischen Eismeer und Sahara*, Stuttgart, 1974.

30 Harrison E Salisbury, *The Siege of Leningrad*, p.476, Secker and Warburg, London, 1969.

31 Revd A P Wales, in Eric Taylor, *Heroines of World War Two*, Robert Hale, London, 1991.

32 Lettice Curtis, cited in Jonathan Croall, *Don't You Know There's a War On?*, p.67, Hutchinson, London, 1988.

33 Galina Vishnevskaya, *Galina*, p.46, Sceptre Books, London, 1984.

34 Cited in Salisbury, *op. cit.*, p.173.

35 Lieut. Juanita Redmond, *I served on Bataan*, p.40, J B Lippincott, Philadelphia and New York 1943.

36 *Ibid.*, p.74.

37 Cited in Taylor, *op. cit.*

38 Abie Abrahams, *Ghost of Bataan Speaks*, p.15, Vintage Press, New York, 1971.

39 Cited in Flower and Reeves, *op. cit.*, p.276, from Walter Millis, *This is Pearl*, William Morrow, 1947.

40 Abrahams, *op. cit.*, p.241.

41 Louise Reed Spencer, cited in *Guerrilla Wife*, pp.82–3, Thomas Crowell, New York, 1944.

42 Colonel Masonubu Tsuji, *Singapore: The Japanese Version*, translated by Margaret Lake, R Smith, Halstead Press, Australia, 1960.

43 Cited in Flower and Reeves, *op. cit.*, p.718; from Lieutenant-General Robert L Eichelberger, *Jungle Road to Tokyo*, Odhams Press, London, 1951.

44 Cited in Flower and Reeves, *op. cit.*, p.718; from Eichelberger, *op. cit.*

45 Cited in Flower and Reeves, *op. cit.*, p.726; from Major-General Chas A Willoughby and John Chamberlain, *MacArthur, 1941–45: Victory in the Pacific*, Heinemann, 1956.

46 Cited in Saburo Ienaga, *Japan's Last War*, p.126, Blackwell, London, 1979.

47 Ienaga, *op. cit.*, p.221.

48 Allen Dulles, in Flower and Reeves, *op. cit.*, p.929; from Allen Dulles, *Germany's Underground*, Macmillan, New York, 1947.

49 James Bacque, *Other Losses*, Macdonald, London, 1989.

50 Gwen Terasaki, in Flower and Reeves, *op. cit.*; from Terasaki, *op.cit.*

51 Cited in Flower and Reeves, *op. cit.*, p.1031; from Marcel Junod, *Warrior Without Weapons*, Jonathan Cape, London, 1951.

52 Gwen Terasaki, cited in Flower and Reeves, *op. cit.*; from Terasaki, *op. cit.*

Acknowledgements

For permission to reprint copyright material the publishers gratefully acknowledge the following: Aitken & Stone Ltd for R M Wingfield, *Only Way Out*; BBC Enterprises for Patricia Williams (ed), *Children at War*; Blackwell Publishers for Saburo Ienaga, *Japan's Last War*; Bloomsbury Publishing (and the CBF World Jewish Relief as copyright holders) for Barry Turner, *And the Policeman Smiled*; Curtis Brown Ltd for Harrison Salisbury, *The Siege of Leningrad*, and for Gwen Terasaki, *Bridge to the Sun*; Faber and Faber Ltd for Pascal Jardin, *Vichy Boyhood*; Excerpt from *Galina – A Russian Story*, English translation copyright © 1984 by Galina Vishnevskaya reprinted by permission Harcourt Brace Jovanovich, Inc. and Hodder and Stoughton Ltd; Harper-Collins Publishers for P Hallie, *Lest Innocent Blood be Shed*, and for Anton Gill, *The Journey Back from Hell* (Grafton Books, 1986, an imprint of HarperCollins); Holocaust Publications for Alexander Donat, *Holocaust Kingdom*; The Controller of Her Majesty's Stationery Office for *Trial of Major German War Criminals*; Jonathan Cape for Jonathan Croall, *Don't You Know There's a War On*, and for Marcel Junod, *Warrior Without Weapons*; Little Brown and Co (UK) for James Bacque, *Other Losses*; Macmillan Publishing Co for Allen Dulles, *Germany's Underground*; Martin Secker and Warburg for Milton Shulman, *Defeat in the West*; Nelson Blackie for Caws and Watts (eds), *Earthquake Hour*; Octopus for Major-General Chas Willoughby and John Chamberlain, *Victory in the Pacific*; Oxford University Press for Bernard Wasserstein, *Britain and the Jews of Europe, 1939–45*; Penguin Books Ltd (and the Trustees of the Mass Observation Archive as copyright holders) for Dorothy Barton, *Living Through the Blitz*, and Penguin Books Ltd for Livingston, Moore and Oldfather, The Japan Reader, Vol. 1; Peters Fraser and Dunlop Group Ltd for Guy Chapman, *Vain Glory*; Random House, Inc. for John Dower, *War Without Mercy*; Robert Hale Ltd for Eric Taylor, *Heroines of World War II*; Mrs Carol Wain for D Hornsey, *Here Today Bomb Tomorrow*.

While every effort has been made to secure permission, in some cases it has proved impossible to trace the copyright holders. The publishers apologise for this apparent negligence.

Index